W9-BLV-634

"I was delighted that Christopher Ash's new book unpacks the overlooked exhortation of Hebrews 13 v 17—namely, that it is the responsibility of the sheep to make the shepherd's work a joy and not a burden. Christopher lays out seven ways to do so. I know of no other book like this—it is a 'charge to the congregation' that is more specific and practical than anything else you will find in print."

TIMOTHY KELLER, Pastor Emeritus, Redeemer Presbyterian Church, New York City

"Too many pastors today are discouraged, isolated and weary, and it shows in the alarming rate of drop-out from pastoral ministry. Christopher Ash has pooled his extensive experience and wisdom to produce a book that could help make a real difference. If church members and leadership teams can read this book, we could help more pastors persevere and thrive in their ministry to us."

MICHAEL REEVES, President and Professor of Theology, Union School of Theology

"In the short time it will take to read this book, a radical shift may well take place—a shift in orientation from asking, 'How is my pastor doing in meeting my needs?' to 'How am I doing in caring for my pastor?'"

NANCY GUTHRIE, Author and Bible teacher

"Christopher Ash has served churches well for decades. Now he provides a most unusual service: a modern take on an old form—the church member's handbook. Christopher has asked the simple question 'How can I love and serve my pastor in a way that will do him, his family and our church good?' The answer is straightforward, biblical and life-giving. Careful and loving, this in fact *is* a book your pastor wishes you would read (but we *are* too embarrassed to ask you). Thanks, Christopher!"

MARK DEVER, Pastor, Capitol Hill Baptist, Washington, DC

"This book will help church members understand Scripture better so that they become better able to meet pastors in their need. After all, don't you want their work to be a joy, not a burden (Hebrews 13 v 17)—a joy and not a burden both to them and to the sheep in their flock? I wonder how much the fruitful and happy functioning of a local church turns on believers who are grateful encouragers of their pastors—prayerful warriors who draw out from their under-shepherd the very best he can give them!"

D.A. CARSON, Research Professor of New Testament, Trinity Evangelical Divinity School; President, The Gospel Coalition

"We know that pastors care for the church, but who cares for pastors? The church does! Let Christopher Ash introduce you to a new category: caring for your pastor so your pastor can happily care for you."

C.J. MAHANEY, Senior Pastor, Sovereign Grace Church of Louisville

"Christopher's usual clear teaching is shared through countless stories and illustrations from ministers' lives. He tackles a vital subject we often skirt around, and earths it with practical ideas, questions and prayers. Find someone not too embarrassed to promote it in your church!"

HUGH & CLARE PALMER, All Souls, Langham Place, London

"The best thing about this book is that it will make your church 'do church' better. Christopher's penetrating insights will raise the bar for all Christians. We can't wait for our whole church to read this!"

DENESH & DEBORAH DIVYANATHAN, The Crossing Church, Singapore

"I'm hugely grateful for this vital and vibrant little tonic for maintaining healthy relationships between pastors and their congregations."

RICHARD COEKIN, Executive Director, Co-Mission, London

"Christopher Ash has an extraordinary ability to identify books which need to be written and then write them! We all need biblical encouragement, and this will help people provide their ministers with much-needed support and encouragement. Praise God for this useful book!"

PETER ADAM, Vicar Emeritus, St Jude's Carlton, Melbourne; Former Principal, Ridley College, Melbourne

"A wonderfully encouraging, challenging, wise and readable book. It is not only a book your pastor wishes you would read but one that this pastor's wife highly recommends too."

CLARE HEATH-WHYTE, Author, *Old Wives' Tales* and *Everyone A Child Should Know*

"We greatly appreciate this important and timely book—full of biblical wisdom and practical counsel about how church members and pastors should relate to and encourage one another as together they grow in Christ. A book to be widely read and shared—for the good health of our churches."

JOHN & MOYA WOODHOUSE, Sydney, Australia

"All of us will do well to heed the wise biblical counsel of this brief book. Our pastors will be better for it—and so will our churches."

JONATHAN GRIFFITHS, Lead Pastor, Metropolitan Bible Church, Ottawa, Canada

"We were challenged and encouraged afresh to have soft hearts and to engage humbly and wholeheartedly in our local church family—and cannot think of anyone who wouldn't be helped and challenged by reading this book."

GARY & FIONA MILLAR, Queensland Theological College, Brisbane, Australia

"Christopher Ash has a knack of putting his finger on the sensitive nerve-endings of churches and their pastors. This book is no exception. If we 'read, mark, learn and inwardly digest' these pages, both our churches and our ministers will be healthier and happier."

SINCLAIR B. FERGUSON, Ligonier Teaching Fellow and Chancellor's Professor of Systematic Theology, Reformed Theological Seminary

"Some churches support their leaders well but others do not. Some energise their leaders successfully but others suck the life out of them! So how are we to encourage our leaders and make their work a joy rather than a burden? With clarity and insight, Christopher shows us what to do and why it's in our best interests to do that!"

CARRIE SANDOM, Director of Women's Ministry, The Proclamation Trust, London

"The shepherd tends the flock—we get that—but whoever thought of the flock looking after the shepherd?! Christopher Ash did and, with his usual clarity and kindness, he shows us what that means and why it matters."

ALISTAIR BEGG, Senior Pastor, Parkside Church, Cleveland, Ohio; Bible teacher, Truth for Life

"Where do you get people who know how to pastor their pastor and (in doing so) make him a better pastor? You could wait for them to appear or you could give out this book in great quantities. It will make pastors weep for joy that someone understands, and will make people wise for action of the most useful kind. We loved it."

SIMON & KATHY MANCHESTER, St Thomas' Anglican Church, North Sydney

"We found this book both practical and encouraging. There is no doubt that those who read this will be strengthened in their discipleship, and their pastor hugely encouraged."

NAT & HELEN SCHLUTER, Johannesburg Bible College

Christopher Ash

THE BOOK YOUR PASTOR
WISHES
YOU WOULD
READ

(but is too embarrassed to ask)

thegoodbook
COMPANY

The book your pastor wishes you would read
(but is too embarrassed to ask)
© Christopher Ash 2019

Published by:
The Good Book Company

thegoodbook.com | www.thegoodbook.co.uk
thegoodbook.com.au | thegoodbook.co.nz | thegoodbook.co.in

ISBN: 9781784983635 | Printed in India

Design by André Parker

Contents

Introduction

Why would your pastor be embarrassed to ask you to read this book? Because it tells you how to care for them.

Surely that's the wrong way around. When a friend asked me what I was writing, I explained that I was trying to write a book about how we care for our pastors. "But surely," she said, "they are supposed to care for us, aren't they?!"

You do need your pastor to look after you, and so do I. I need, and I deeply appreciate, those who care for me pastorally, who keep watch over my soul, who love me and pray for me, counsel me and preach to me. But what's all this about me caring for them?

From me to you

I want to write to you, as one church member to another, and not to write to your pastor. There is a place for speaking to the church leader, and plenty of books and talks at ministry conferences do that. But I want to speak to *you*, an ordinary church member like me. I want to speak to you about how to care for your pastor.

You may call your church leader a pastor, a minister, or something else. You may, if you belong to a larger church, have other staff on the church payroll—perhaps an assistant pastor, a women's pastoral worker, a youth minister and so on. If so, include them in your thoughts.

I want you to read this book. I want that very much. I want it because it's important. And precisely because your pastor will be embarrassed to ask you. But you should. You will be a better Christian in a better church if you do. What I write about is very important and widely neglected. You may not have thought about it; but I hope you will now.

Our pastors will be embarrassed to ask because I'm going to consider how we can care for them better. Even though what I will say is what the Bible teaches, it is not easy for your own pastor to give you a message that amounts to this: "Come on, guys, you need to raise your game!" If they are not embarrassed, they probably should be! So I'm going to do it for them.

I'm going to do this because I know what being a pastor is like and what being a church member is like—because I was a pastor, and I am now a church member. I was a pastor for over eleven years, first as an assistant in a large city-centre church and then as the pastor of a smaller village church-plant. I then served for eleven years as Director of the Proclamation Trust's Cornhill Training Course in London. Since 2015, I have been Writer-in-Residence at Tyndale House in Cambridge, UK.

As a pastor, I was very well looked after, so I have no sour grapes and no axe to grind. Then, in my role with the Proclamation Trust and associated networks, I was brought into contact with lots of pastors and pastors-in-training, and plenty of churches. So I've seen what happens when this goes wrong—but also how churches flourish when it goes wonderfully right. And I'm now a church member, who needs to think just as carefully about these things as I'm hoping you will.

You may think you don't need to read this book. But you do. We all need to look after our pastors and—paradoxically—it is in our own best interests to do so. If you and I do not care for our pastors, then they will not be able to care for us. I want to warn you about how it can go horribly wrong. But, above all,

I want to set before you a healthy two-way dynamic in which pastors care for people and people care for pastors; and both pastors and people grow in a glad Christ-likeness.

And that's the kind of church we'd all like to be part of.

PASTORS ARE PEOPLE TOO
A tour of the pastors' hall of faith

Before we think together about caring for our pastors, I want to take a step back and help us think about something very obvious but easily neglected: our pastors are people. Well, you say, of course they are; I knew that. Yes, but it is easy to forget. It is natural to think about our pastors in terms of *what they do*—how they lead and pray and preach and teach and so on; but what about *who they are*? We tend to see our pastors at their most polished. I want us to see them, or at least imagine them, as they are.

So come with me to the pastors' hall of faith. I want to introduce you to ten pastors. They are not paintings or statues; each of them is alive and sitting at their desk on the same Monday morning. They have had the same Sunday. The same people came to church, listened (or did not listen) to their ministry, mingled, chatted, prayed, grumbled, were thankful, sang, were morose or thoughtful, came to the pastor with the same intractable pastoral problems, shared an answer to prayer, brought some enquirers to church (or didn't), and so on. The same Sunday. And now it is Monday morning.

I am going to tell you something about each one. Not everything—very far from everything—but something that has shaped them to be the pastor they are. And something that will affect how they responded to that Sunday and how they are as they face this Monday. For their thoughts, their mood, their feelings, their energy or lack of energy, their enthusiasm or weariness, are all affected not only by what happened on Sunday but by who they are.

Does this seem an absurd experiment? Perhaps. And yet I think you will find, by the time you have walked around this hall of faith, that it may help you to think of your pastor as a human being, perhaps in a way you have never done before. Try it and see.

There is no particular agenda in these fictional cameos. Their only aim is to spur you to think about pastors as people.

—

Andy's father was a skilled craftsman. Practical work—the ability to make things well and make things work—was highly valued in their childhood home. Often, Andy's dad would show him, with justifiable pride, some finished artefact or completed project. Andy did an apprenticeship as a builder; he developed some skill and really enjoyed being able to finish a building project and look at the end product. "By God's grace, I made that, built that, finished that," he would say to himself, with thanks in his heart towards God.

But then Andy left and went into the "wordy" world of pastoral ministry. It's a very different world. He can never look on a completed pastoral task the way his father could look at a finished piece of craftsmanship. He thinks over yesterday's conversations: the loose ends of men's and women's lives, the half-healed and yet half-dissolving marriages, the hopeful signs of faith spoiled by depressing symptoms of unbelief, the sheer unfinishedness of pastoral work. He longs to *finish* something, really finish it; but he knows that, for all his completed outward tasks—the sermon preached, the elders' meeting chaired, the pastoral visit made—the tasks that really fill his day are never finished.

———

Ben came to Christ as a student in a large, young, vibrant city-centre church where he then served as an apprentice. The preaching and teaching of the pastors impacted him profoundly, as did the one-to-one Bible-reading times with a student worker on the church staff. These were his role models for fruitful ministry. When challenged to consider pastoral ministry, it was these lives and examples that inspired him, and he could think of nothing better than to be like them.

Yesterday seemed very different. The church he serves does not sparkle with life. Far from it. The people are quite, well, ordinary. There doesn't seem to be a huge amount going on. The music is a bit dull. Talent is in short supply. Oh, sure, he prays, he preaches, he meets people one to one, he pays pastoral visits and teaches the Bible to people. But it doesn't feel at all like that city-centre church where he began.

—

Colin was from a Christian home. In fact, his father had left his secular job to train for pastoral ministry in midlife. His parents were thrilled when Colin followed in his father's footsteps, and have not stopped saying so. They can think of no higher calling for their son. Like many proud parents, they have high expectations

THE BOOK YOUR PASTOR WISHES YOU WOULD READ

and exalted hopes for him—of wide, deep and lasting influence for Christ.

It is a wonderful legacy that Colin enjoys from his parents. And yet, as he sits at his desk putting the realities of yesterday side by side with these expectations, he cannot but be thoughtful. What does wide, deep and lasting influence for Christ mean in the week-by-week realities of pastoral life? Mostly—and yesterday was no exception—he feels he is having close to zero real influence for Christ. His vision is filled with frustrations—the man who will not repent, the comfortable couple full of grumbles, the young woman scarred by what has been said and done to her in the past, the teenager gripped by enslaving addiction.

———

Deepak came from a culture where an academically capable son was expected to qualify in some prestigious and well-paid profession, usually as a doctor or lawyer. He is clever and capable. His dad and mum hoped for just this from him as they supported him through his education; and they made their expectations very clear. He did qualify as a lawyer and practised law for a few years.

But then Deepak left to enter pastoral ministry. It's a very different world. He can't help comparing the two spheres. As he sits at his pastor's desk on Monday morning, he remembers the prestigious surroundings of his law firm, the sense of significance and the little markers of status that he used to know. The inadequate church building, the rather tatty décor, the absence of colleagues (let alone juniors to command), the loneliness—they begin to get to him and lower his spirits. Has he been wise to give up *that* for *this*?

—

Ethan was brought up in a Christian home in a small rural church, where he saw unimpressive but faithful ministry bear fruit in slowly changed lives. For him, this is the ideal to which he aspires. He cannot think of anything more worthwhile than the quiet, steady work of getting alongside men and women in the stabilities of rural life, teaching them the gospel of Jesus, praying for and with them, year after year after year.

Somehow, it fits quite well with yesterday. Ethan sits at his desk quietly contented and settles to another day of prayer and preparing to teach the Bible.

—

Finn has been a rootless millennial. His experience of Christian ministry has been overwhelmingly through the podcasts of famous preachers on the internet. His mind is filled with images of well-known speakers on screens teaching at large conferences. Finn doesn't have any authentic first-hand knowledge of local church ministry that has impressed him. So, as he mulls on yesterday, the humdrum life of his local church feels like a parallel universe compared with the big-name speakers on bright platforms speaking eloquently to large crowds. He just feels a bit lost in the little world of the local church he serves.

As he sits at his desk, he is not quite sure how to sort out in his mind the maelstrom of experiences from yesterday—all the different conversations with people of different ages and stages of life, with such a myriad of varied challenges in their lives. It's all very new to him, and he feels he needs the spiritual equivalent of a caffeine hit from some famous preacher.

—

Gerald went to one of the top schools in his country. The family home was quite an impressive pile. Both mum and dad ran good cars. Money was never in short supply. Holidays were comfortable, sometimes quite exotic affairs; his clothes were new and fashionable, with designer labels; gadgets and gizmos were up-to-the-minute and replaced with the newest model frequently.

Now he's on the staff team of a large inner-city church. It's a great work and he loves seeing local people being reached for Jesus. But Gerald can't help struggling to get used to the drab surroundings, the very low income and the constant struggle to make ends meet. He doesn't resent it; he knows it's a sacrifice worth making; but it is so different to his childhood and it just is hard.

—

Harry is a voracious reader but he is shy; he prefers his own company when he wants to replenish his emotional batteries. He can manage the public role of a pastor and being among a large group, but the experience drains him a lot more than it does his extrovert friends. When the diary gets too crowded, he struggles with a kind of emotional and psychological claustrophobia and longs for some space—physical space, time space, personal space, aloneness space.

After a busy Sunday he feels very squeezed. Harry preached at the two morning services, with what felt like hundreds of snippets of conversations before, between, and afterwards. He and his wife hosted two young families, a young couple, a widow and two singles for lunch. And then he led the evening service and interviewed some mission partners in a meeting for the 20s and 30s after church, before sitting at the back for the end of the youth-group meeting, to mix with the teenagers. He sits at his desk on this Monday morning just staring emptily into space…

———

Ian's wife, Imogen, was a high-earning banker in the central business district of their capital city. When she married Ian, he too was doing well in finance. Then they had children, and Imogen decided to work in the home as a full time, hard working but unpaid mother. That was fine, while Ian brought home good pay. And then Ian left to become a pastor. However keen a Christian she may be, Imogen would scarcely be human if she did not feel the financial draught.

As Ian sits at his desk, he knows he should be praying and preparing with his Bible open. But he can't help coming back in his mind to the painful conversation he and Imogen had last night about not being able to afford a summer holiday.

———

Jez is a preacher's kid. Brought up simply, with enough but rarely more than enough. Holidays were simple affairs, camping not too far from home. The family car was bruised and battered, if much loved. Shoes and clothes were, more often than not, hand-me-downs. It wasn't easy, and there were anxieties about money; but there always seemed to be enough.

He's a pastor now and loving it. There's not much money, and he and his fiancée wonder quite how they will make ends meet when they marry in the autumn. But it's a great life, and he is overwhelmed with the privilege of bringing the good news of Jesus to the people in his care. He sits at his desk praying for one and another with a deep thankfulness in his heart.

———

And now you come to your own pastor as they sit at their desk in the pastors' hall of faith. What might be going on in their mind and heart this Monday morning? For God has entrusted them with this work in the concrete reality of all their history, their personality, their interests and their circumstances—in all the strange mix that is their full humanity.

That's the pastor you need to care for.

A prayer

Father God, thank you that the Lord Jesus, your Son, the great Shepherd of the sheep, was and is fully a human being, with human thoughts and feelings. Thank you that he has appointed under-shepherds, pastors, and that they too are fully human beings. Grant that I may pray for those who pastor me, understanding a little more of their struggles, hopes and fears. For Jesus' sake, Amen.

Why would you want to care for your pastor?

Have confidence in your leaders and submit to their authority, because they keep watch over you as those who must give an account. Do this so that their work will be a joy, not a burden, for that would be of no benefit to you.

Hebrews 13 v 17

J osh and Ashley belong to the same church. They meet on Monday in the shopping mall. Ashley says she is just taking a letter round to their pastor to thank him—with some chocolates!—for yesterday's sermon. It was so helpful to her and Mike, her fiancé, in their walk with Christ, and it reminded them of how much they owe to their pastor's patient preaching and teaching week by week. She thought he looked a bit down yesterday, and figured he could use some encouragement.

Josh responds politely but is rather surprised. He was actually thinking the opposite before he bumped into Ashley. He and his wife Heather had been talking together at breakfast about their disappointment that the pastor hadn't visited or looked after them after Heather's recent miscarriage. They feel a bit sore that the pastor is not caring for them. Nothing could be further from their minds than wondering how they could care for the pastor.

—

Why would you want to care for your pastor? Unless you and I are motivated really to want to care for our pastors, we won't pay much attention to what's in this book.

So let's begin with asking how we might reasonably hope that our pastors will care for us. We may hope for all sorts of things. But what does the Bible encourage us to hope for. In brief, there are five key ways:

How do we hope our pastors will care for us?

First, we may reasonably hope that they will *preach to us the gospel message of life in Jesus*. At the end of the letter to the Hebrews, the writer describes church leaders as those "who spoke the word of God to you" (Hebrews 13 v 7). The Bible means by this more than just factual teaching; it includes pressing the message home with repeated urgency, applying it with insight to our hearts and wills, and teaching us the whole will of God (Acts 20 v 27—the whole of God's purpose and plan).

I hope my pastor will preach to me with such depth of insight into the things of God, such wise knowledge of the human condition, and such perceptive reflections on contemporary culture that, as I sit under such preaching, my heart will be warmed, my mind instructed, my will challenged, my sinfulness exposed, and my whole worldview be deeply and lastingly converted. That will stretch the energies of the most gifted of pastors; it is no light work.

Second, and inseparably related to the preaching, we may hope that our pastors will *pray for us*. Their ministry is modelled upon the leadership ministries of the apostles, who describe it as "prayer and the ministry of the word" (Acts 6 v 4). Part of the apostles' ministry was unique and unrepeatable, for they testified as eyewitnesses who had seen, heard, looked upon and touched the incarnate Son of God, in his earthly ministry and, supremely, in his resurrection (1 John 1 v 1-3).

Pastoral ministry today cannot be eyewitness ministry in this unrepeatable way. But it should be apostolic as a ministry shaped by prayer and the ministry of the word. Prayer here means—as it meant for the prophets and for the Lord Jesus—a particular burden to pray for the people to whom they preach.

We therefore hope that our pastors will take upon themselves the burden of knowing us sufficiently well, and caring for us with enough depth, to pray for us individually, as each of us has need. That will stretch the energies of the most spiritual of pastors; it is no light work.

By the way, if your church is large, it may be unrealistic to expect your pastor to know each individual well. If so, it is their responsibility to delegate to other leaders or elders, so that everyone in the church is known well, and prayed for individually, by at least one of them. Moses did something similar when he found the people of God were too numerous for him to care for by himself (Exodus 18 v 13-26).

Delegation is evidence that our pastors do care for us, not that they don't.

Third, we hope they will *keep careful watch over our lives.* Later in Hebrews 13, the writer describes the leaders as those who "keep watch over you" (Hebrews 13 v 17). Like the prophet Ezekiel with the people of God in an earlier age (Ezekiel 34), our pastors are to be watchmen, keeping careful watch for the wolves who lurk in the dark borders around the sheepfold of Christ's flock, watching us for signs of sliding back into our former lives, guarding us against the dangers of the world, the flesh and the devil. We hope they will know us sufficiently well, and individually, to be able to do this with care, insight and faithfulness. That will stretch the capacities of the most energetic and empathetic of pastors; it is no light work.

Fourth, our pastor-teachers are given to us by the ascended Christ in order to *equip us* so that we can all live lives of active and fruitful service of Jesus. In Ephesians 4 v 11-13, Paul writes that "Christ himself gave the apostles, the prophets"—two unique and foundational gifts, as Ephesians 2 v 20 and 3 v 5 make clear—and also "the evangelists, the pastors and teachers" (or "pastor-teachers") "to equip his people for works of service".

By teaching us, by preaching to us, by praying for us, and by watching over us, our pastors lead us into maturity in Christ, so that we may serve as each of us is individually gifted to do. This equipping is not so much a matter of imparting skills (which is what we tend to think "training" is about), but about leading us into lives of godliness and mature understanding in Christ. It is a spiritual matter more than a functional task. Such an equipping will stretch the strongest pastor to their limits; it is no light work.

Finally, we may reasonably hope that they will *lead the church well*. Paul writes of elders (i.e. leaders) "who direct the affairs of the church well" (1 Timothy 5 v 17). They serve Christ by leading his people; they serve us by leading us. If they lead badly, our churches will suffer, which is why the pastoral letters (1 and 2 Timothy and Titus) have so much to say about the high qualifications of the men who led the churches. If they lead well, much blessing follows. But bearing the burden and care of a church—let alone the burden and care of many churches, as Paul did—is a task that will take the most experienced and zealous pastor to the very edge of their abilities; it is no light work.

It is no surprise, perhaps, that the Bible compares a church leader to a hard-working ox on a farm

(1 Timothy 5 v 18). It is not a flattering or glamorous metaphor; but it catches the sheer hard work involved in fulfilling what God calls a pastor to do.

How can a pastor be motivated to do all this?

We might want to say that motivating the pastor is up to them; they need to find motivation from the depths of their own souls, from their own walk with the Lord Jesus, or—failing that—from their fellow pastors or perhaps a more senior pastor. All that may be true. But the surprising answer the Bible gives is that *we*, the ordinary church members, are the ones who can motivate our pastors. The rest of this book considers how.

What will motivate a pastor not only to begin this work but to persevere in it with patient endurance, never turning his hand from the plough? The answer—or a serious part of the answer—comes most surprisingly in a verse we have already glanced at, in Hebrews 13 v 17. "Have confidence in your leaders and submit to their authority," writes the author of the letter, "because they keep watch over you as those who must give an account". It is what he says next that is so surprising: "Do this so that their work will be a joy, not a burden, for that would be of no benefit *to you.*" Just look at those last two words: "to you". I can see that making their work a joy will be good *for them*, and that if it is a burden, it will be tough *for them*. But *for us?!* How so?

Answer: unless there is at least some whisper of joy in their hearts as they do their work, some spring of gladness in their step, they will never persevere to the end. And—and this is the point—it is we who will suffer. Instead of being well taught—faithfully preached to with insight and depth—instead of being patiently prayed for, instead of having our souls guarded from evil, instead of being lovingly equipped, instead of being well led in our churches, we will be harassed and helpless, like sheep without a shepherd, at the mercy of all kinds of destructive evil. And our churches will be places of shallow immaturity and instability, at the mercy of every whim of cultural pressure or theological oddity.

It is therefore in our own interests, to say nothing of love for the pastor, that we should make their work a joy and not simply a heavy and gloomy burden. If you and I truly grasp the extent to which healthy pastoral oversight is a team effort—a two-way dynamic in which we, as church members, play as critical a part as our pastors—then, and only then, will we be urgently motivated to learn the better to care for them. You and I have it in our power to demotivate our pastors, so that they are gradually ground down into a slough of despond from which they will be utterly unable to do us any good at all. But we also have it in our power so to cheer them, so to put a spring in their step, that they will gladly do for us all that we hope and pray.

In the following chapters we look at seven virtues that we as church members can learn, and that can make our pastor's work a joy. For each virtue, we will also take a look at the dark side, the corresponding vice that will drain our pastors of joy. Let's pray that thinking about these virtues and vices will help each one of us to be a church member who brings joy to our pastor's heart and so, in turn, helps them to love and serve us better.

A prayer

Father God, I do not know whether the work of watching over my soul is a joyful privilege or a heavy burden to my pastor. If I have made it a heavy burden by my hard-heartedness, my impenitence, my spiritual apathy or my rebelliousness, I repent. Please change my heart and make me the kind of zealous, humble, shiningly Christ-like believer for whom to care is a great joy. For Jesus' sake, Amen.

SEVEN VIRTUES
of church members
that impact our pastors

1. Daily repentance and eager faith

A pastor's visits one week included these two.
The first was to a home where all was well. Ryan and Steph were prosperous; the home was pleasant; a good car sat on the driveway; the children were being educated in expensive schools; their manners were good; talent abounded.

The second was to a single mum. Nicole had been abandoned some years before by an abusive husband; she was bringing up Dan and Jim, two very difficult boys, alone; and she herself struggled with serious and persistent health troubles.

The pastor went away downcast and discouraged after one visit, thrilled and energised after the other. But which was which?

—

That pastor was me (although I have changed the names). Which visit cheered me more? I remember well. I came home from the first—where everything was "fine"—deeply depressed; and from the second walking on air. How come?

Ryan and Steph conformed outwardly to Christian beliefs, but showed no sense of deep heart work, no feeling that they really wanted to be wholehearted disciples of Jesus—in a word, no evidence of genuine repentance and lively faith. But, in the second, although the problems were crushing—and I did feel the pain of them—in Nicole's heart there was a joy in the Lord Jesus, a quiet determination to walk with him through whatever life had in store, and a gritty and very real trust.

The very best thing you can do for your pastor, and I for mine, is to repent daily of sin and trust afresh daily in Jesus. To be honest, if you and I do this—together with the second virtue (page 47)—even if we are terrible at looking after our pastors in other ways, they will probably keep on pastoring year after year.

Walking in the truth

In the short letters we call 2 John and 3 John, the elderly apostle John writes twice about the joy that comes to a pastor's heart when they hear this kind of news:

> *It has given me **great joy** to find some of your children* [that is, members of your church] *walking in the truth.*   2 John v 4

> *It gave me **great joy** when some believers came and testified about your faithfulness to the truth, telling how you continue to walk in it. I have **no greater joy** than to hear that my children* [men and women under my pastoral care] *are walking in the truth.*   3 John v 3-4

To "walk in the truth" means much the same as to "walk in the light" (1 John 1 v 7). This does not, of course, mean achieving sinless perfection. Rather, it means a regular confession of sin and repentance, so that the direction of our lives keeps turning back towards God's law and God's ways. And it means a clear and fresh trust that Jesus saves us from our sins. John makes all this clear in 1 John 1 v 5 – 2 v 2.

This gives a pastor joy because it's the reason they came into pastoral ministry. Whatever work they may have left behind them, they became a pastor because they dream and yearn and long that men and women should bring honour to God by walking in the truth, by following Jesus with fresh faith and honest repentance, as they themselves seek to do. If men and women are doing this under their ministry, they can wake up in the morning and get out of bed with a spring in their step. Nothing so drains a pastor of vital energy as having to preach to, having to go on praying for, having to try to lead and care for men and women who are impervious to the good news of God's grace. Hardness of heart is the great pastor-killer.

How to bring your pastor joy

Walking in the truth will mean demonstrating an eagerness to know our Bibles, to go on and on learning and grasping truth with fresh depth. Luke writes with delight about the Jewish people in Berea who received Paul's gospel message "with great eagerness and examined the Scriptures every day to see if what Paul said was true" (Acts 17 v 11). They really wanted to know. Perhaps they went on and on reading their Bibles eagerly day after day, long after they had come to faith in Christ.

In sad contrast, the writer of the letter to the Hebrews laments that his readers have become dull of heart and lazy. He so wants to explain a wonderful truth about Jesus to them, but he can't help wondering if there is any point in trying. "We have much to say," he writes, "but it is hard to make it clear"—not because the truths are particularly difficult but "because you no longer try to understand" (Hebrews 5 v 11).

This lazy approach to Bible teaching, Bible reading and Bible learning—then as now—is not a matter of low academic ability. They (we) may be very clever and highly educated. Back in the 4th century, plenty of very ordinary North Africans stood for a couple of hours to hear Augustine open up the word of God to them! No, the hearts of those to whom Hebrews is written are hardened; that is why they are lazy.

Few things so encourage a pastor as eager listeners and learners. "I am so looking forward to Sunday's sermon!" I remember a church member saying this to me, and the effect on my prayer and preparation was electric: "If they are so eager to hear, the least I can do is get out of bed in the morning and labour hard at the word, so there is something worth hearing!"

One old Christian used to say that one of the best sounds a preacher could hear was the rustle of Bible pages as people eagerly turned up the Bible passage, ready to listen.

A friend, serving in what is mostly a deeply discouraging church, comments that "there is one lady who always thanks me after every sermon for encouraging her in the Lord". What a difference that makes!

But it will take more than just the rustle of pages. We will encourage our pastors if our hunger for the word of God is not simply a hunger to hear but also an eagerness to "do what it says". We won't be like those who look in a mirror, see how dirty they are, and then go away unwashed. Rather, we will long to change and be changed by God's Spirit working through God's word (James 1 v 22-25).

But what if a sermon isn't very good?

What if our pastors have not preached or taught very well? It does happen; those of us who have been pastors ruefully remember preaching badly all too often and, for some of us, all too recently.

I am not talking about false teaching. If our pastor preaches a *false* gospel—a so-called gospel that is not the true gospel of Jesus—then we are not to encourage them. Rather we are to seek to correct them and, if they refuse to be corrected, we are to do all we can to remove them from their pastoral position. Failing that, we must leave their church.

No, I am talking about when they preach and teach faithfully, but just not very well. Then we are faced with a choice. We can take the easy option, which is to criticise them—to eat roast preacher for dinner; it is much easier to criticise preaching than to do it. Or we can resolutely choose the tougher call, which is to seek to learn from the Bible passage some truth that will move us to a fresh repentance and a fresh faith.

This is a particular challenge for me. For more than a decade, I ran a training course for preachers and Bible teachers, so I am now hard-wired to produce structured criticism of a sermon. I can almost do it in my sleep! But, while there is a place for that—and a wise preacher will ask carefully chosen friends to give that kind of constructive criticism—I will discourage my pastors and damage myself if that is all that I do. Often, if I have listened to a sermon that wasn't great, I read through the Bible passage again and pick perhaps one phrase to take away that will move me to walk in the truth in the week ahead.

Listen up
How can you prepare yourself for Sunday's sermon? It is a good discipline to pray for your pastor each week. Read for yourself the passage they will be preaching.

Pray for their heart, that God may weave the Bible passage not only into their mind but into their heart, their conscience and their feelings. Pray for your own heart, that as you hear the passage preached, God will weave that same passage into your own mind, heart, conscience and feelings.

There is a perennial danger that we will only want to thank a preacher when they have said what we wanted to hear. Back in the Ephesus of the first century, Paul had to warn Timothy that sometimes people will not put up with healthy truth, but instead, "to suit their own desires, they will gather round them [literally "heap up"!] a great number of teachers to say what their itching ears want to hear" (2 Timothy 4 v 3). "Thanks for giving my itching ears a good scratch, pastor. That was just the sort of thing I wanted to hear."

Strangely, that is not encouraging to a faithful pastor, cheering as it may be to a false teacher. Rather, a faithful pastor longs to hear, "Thank you. I didn't find that easy to hear. I don't really want to listen to this. But I know that I need to. And I know it will move me to a healthy change of life. So thank you for having the courage to say it."

It is a tremendous encouragement to our pastors when we thank them for their preaching, their teaching or their personal words of Bible exhortation or comfort. Whether they have preached to us in the main weekly meeting of church or spoken Bible words to us in a small group or just one to one, it is good to learn the habit of thanking them. Not thanking them particularly for their eloquence (if they were eloquent), for their entertainment (if they were entertaining), or even for their manner (if it was winsome), but for the Bible content of what they have taught us.

Being specific about something that helped you will be a particular encouragement to your pastor. Let's see if there is some truth, some verse or some Bible phrase that we will take away from our meeting that will stir us afresh to repent and believe. Then let us tell our pastors about it in a brief word of thanks.

I have often found that a written word of thanks has been of especial encouragement, partly because I can re-read it on bad days, and partly because I can share it with my wife, who is my fellow-worker in the gospel, and she too can be encouraged by this fruit from our shared ministry.

How will you encourage *your* pastor this week, as they open God's word to you?

A prayer

Father God, grant to me an eagerness in hearing your word, a zeal to obey, a glad penitence for sin and determination to live a more godly life this week than last. May it be a great joy to my pastor to see me walking gladly in the truth. For Jesus' sake, Amen.

2. Committed belonging

Matt and Christina have been coming to Christ Church for about five years now. Yesterday they bounced cheerfully up to the pastor after church. "Thanks for the sermon," they said. "We loved that great joke you told." "Do you know Gavin?" asked the pastor, seeking to introduce them to a long-standing member of the church. "No, I don't think so," they said. "But, sorry, got to dash! See you soon." And they were gone. The pastor knew that "soon" likely meant in about four weeks' time.

After Matt and Christina had gone—and it didn't take long—Sheila came up to the pastor. "I don't know if you've met Mel," she said, introducing a middle-aged lady. "I sat next to her today, and she says it's the first time she's come. She's coming back to lunch with me, but I wanted her to meet you."

—

When I was a pastor, I could—very roughly—divide people in church into two categories. There were the people who turned up from time to time, and were often genial, even appreciative, but you knew you might well not see them for a few weeks. And there were the men and women who were there just about every week, and at every prayer meeting.

Here's the test: if you don't see someone at a meeting, do you wonder if they are ill? For the first group, you don't; after all, it is not unusual for them to be absent. For the second, you do; as a responsible pastor you say to yourself, "I didn't see so-and-so in church today; I wonder what has happened."

There is usually some very simple explanation: they were on holiday, or away at a daughter's graduation, or whatever. But you miss them, because you know they are normally there.

Alongside daily personal repentance and fresh personal trust in Jesus (virtue one, page 37) is the shared penitence and faith that are marks of a local church moving towards maturity. Our pastors dream that each man and woman for whom they care will walk in the truth. But they also dream—and in some ways this is even more fundamental to their work—of a local church growing to maturity in Christ.

The book of Ephesians tells us that the victorious and ascended Christ gives pastor-teachers to his church (alongside the foundational apostles and prophets and the ongoing evangelists) for this purpose:

> *… to equip **his people** for works of service, so that **the body of Christ** may be built up until we all reach unity in the faith and in the knowledge of the Son of God and become mature, attaining to the whole measure of the fullness of Christ.* Ephesians 4 v 12-13

The ministry of a pastor is more deeply a ministry to build up the church than it is a ministry to build up individuals. A pastor will therefore rejoice when you and I belong to the local church they serve. (The Bible overview, *Remaking a Broken World*, published by The Good Book Company, will help us see the centrality of the local church in the purposes of God.)

Loving the church like a daughter

It is, I think, very hard, if not impossible, really to feel the pressure of being the leader (or senior pastor) of a local church until you have done it. Even if you have been an associate minister or an assistant pastor, nothing quite prepares you for the day when you are entrusted with senior leadership of a church fellowship, never mind how small and modest that fellowship may be. The responsibility is, in the full sense of the word, awesome. Paul describes it most vividly as being guardian to a virgin daughter, promising her in pure loyalty and devotion to "one husband ... Christ" and caring deeply if she shows any sign of infidelity (2 Corinthians 11 v 2-3).

The anxiety lest the church you lead and serve might "be led astray" from this "sincere and pure devotion to Christ" is comparable to the anxiety of a conscientious guardian of a young woman who shows signs of beginning to sleep around during her engagement; it is that shocking. Try and imagine, for a moment, how that might feel.

No wonder Paul, as the apostolic leader of a wider network of churches, can speak of facing "daily the pressure of my concern for all the churches" (2 Corinthians 11 v 28). In my experience, the daily pressure of concern for one small church was quite enough!

Joy in pastoral ministry is therefore fuelled, perhaps most deeply of all, by signs of a local church who are walking in the truth together. In contrast, one of the most common and most corrosive vices is the Western habit of casual attendance. Of course, it is a good thing that those beginning to sense an interest in the Christian faith can simply attend, with no pressure to do anything more than to watch and listen. But what if this continues after conversion? What if we see church as a provider to meet our needs, rather than a body to which we belong. It may be a provider perhaps of preaching (if it prides itself as a "preaching church"), or of music (if it markets itself as a church where the "worship" is good), or of an experience that makes me feel good, or of a pastoral context in which I will be well loved and cared for.

Whatever it may be, whatever we may seek, the risk is that we regard the church as a provider—a supplier of what we need. So what happens when we move to a new area? First we shop around, sampling the pastoral goods on the shelves of one church after another, and then we attend the one that seems best to meet our particular needs or at least our preferences.

This is especially common in cities, and most of all in city centres; here the church "providers" are most clear in the distinctives of their offerings: "We are a preaching church, you are a worship church, they are a pastoral-care church… Let us each take our pick."

But, of course, when our felt needs change, we will simply leave and start attending somewhere else. Church-shoppers become church-hoppers.

The way we speak of a church is rather like the language we might use of a sports team we support. The transition from "they" to "we" is the big marker. When I first began to follow Swansea City F.C., I used to say, "*They* are in such-and-such a place in the football (soccer) league". But the time needed to come when I said, "*We* are... *We* signed a good striker" (or maybe we didn't). Is there a church you attend or is it a church to which you belong? Is it "they" (or "it") or "we"?

The ministry of turning up
A church in which you include yourself as a member will be a church to which you are committed to turn up Sunday by Sunday. A friend of mine calls this "the ministry of turning up". A former pastor of mine used to suggest that church members did a diary audit, looking over the Sundays of the previous year and counting how many Sundays they were away. I think some of us were rather shocked at how often we had, quite simply, not been there.

Some of our absences were a source of embarrassment to us, purely the seeking of needless pleasure; but there were often lots of honourable reasons for our absence—work commitments, family visits, perhaps even ministry responsibilities. But, whatever the reasons, if we weren't there, how could we possibly encourage one another and stir up one another to love and good works? This is why the writer of the letter to the Hebrews tells his readers not to neglect meeting together "as is the habit of some" (Hebrews 10 v 24-25).

I know of some who actually let their pastor know when they are going to be away: "We are away this Sunday caring for our grandchildren. We shall be praying for you as you preach and for the church as they meet, and we will be sorry to be away." That kind of message demonstrates that we truly regard church as a meeting to which we are committed, and that we miss it only in exceptional circumstances. This will greatly encourage our pastors.

Getting to know you

If simply turning up regularly is one marker of belonging—and one that is hugely encouraging to our pastors—a second marker is that we will invest intentionally in building deep relationships with our brothers and sisters in the church. In some contexts—

especially a large church—this is more of a challenge than in others. We may lament how often we sit next to someone we have never met, have a get-to-know-you starter conversation, and then don't see them again for six months or more. But whatever the context of our church, it will encourage our pastors greatly to see us thinking and then acting intentionally to build deep relationships with a few.

A study of the great "one another" verses in the New Testament can be an inspiring insight into the kinds of honest relationships that should be sought in the local church (for example, Colossians 3 v 5-17). It is worth being resolute about this: perhaps even making a list of the brothers and sisters with whom we will work to develop friendships of care and love that go beyond the superficial.

It will involve taking the hard decision not to build such a relationship with every brother or sister we meet in our church, no matter how delightful or Christ-like they may appear; for we have only so much relational time and emotional energy to invest, and perhaps even less as we get older and already have all manner of such friendships from past churches in other places where we have lived.

The prayer meeting: the best night of the week!

Praying together is a serious mark of belonging. It is good to pray on our own; it is also good, and very natural, and potentially powerful, to pray with our brothers and sisters in Christ. When the apostle Peter was in danger of death, "*the church* was earnestly praying to God for him" (Acts 12 v 5). It is clear they were not praying as separate individuals, but were physically present with one another in one building to pray together (Acts 12 v 12-17).

Our pastors are as deeply encouraged by an eager and active participation in our prayer meetings as they are by our being present on Sundays. Make these a priority, and we will put a spring in the step of our pastors. I remember when a group of members from the church where I served as an assistant moved with me to do a church graft (a plant into a small existing church). One of the things that most encouraged me about those forty or so adults was how, year after year, they were the men and women upon whom I could depend to be there at the church prayer meetings.

If you're not used to being at the prayer meeting, it may seem a little intimidating at first, and you might be nervous about praying aloud in a group. Don't worry. It does get easier after a while, and it's fine simply to sit quietly and pray in your mind. Being there, even if you don't feel able to pray out loud, is what encourages both your pastor and the wider church family.

Lastly, our committed belonging will show itself in a subtle shift of mindset when it comes to our response to the word of God. From my Western individualistic upbringing, my default response to the Bible is individualistic: "*I* am moved to think this, *I* want to act like this, *I* feel this, *I* should respond like this…" It is a remarkable and wonderful shift when I begin to speak of my response as a part of the shared response of my brothers and sisters in our local church: "*We* are learning this from the word of God; *we* need to repent of that sin; *we* are being moved more earnestly to feel this; the word of God is moving *us* in such-and-such a way."

Let us be gladly committed members of our churches; let us flee from the shallow, ephemeral life of the church-shopper (who becomes a church-hopper) or the ecclesiastical spectator. You and I have no idea just what a motivating effect our simple regular presence can have on our pastors. Let's do that for them.

A prayer

Father God, I thank you for the prayerful care that my pastor shows towards my local church, for the way they guard us from spiritual disloyalty to Christ, and for the burden of leadership that they shoulder. Thank you for them. Give them, I pray, the encouragement of seeing men and women truly belonging to the church, serving within the church, and committed to building relationships with brothers and sisters in the church. Please help me to be part of that encouragement by my commitment to the church family. For Jesus' sake, Amen.

3. Open honesty

"How are things?" the pastor asked Josh after the prayer meeting last Wednesday. "Oh, fine, thanks. All fine," replied Josh with an easy smile. Josh was one of the pillars of the church. The pastor could rely on him—he was trustworthy, gifted, generous and willing to serve. Everybody thought well of him.

And then, that very weekend, the pastor heard through the grapevine that Josh had left his wife, Rachel, and gone off with the woman who had, it now transpired, been a secret mistress for five years. Gradually it all came out: how Josh and Rachel had struggled privately with serious difficulties right from the start of their marriage. But nobody else knew. Until now, when it was much too late.

—

Tony and Adam were having roast pastor for lunch. Tony began by criticising the pastor for dull preaching. Adam chimed in, praising the previous pastor—who was so much better, more gifted, more successful… And so the conversation heated up into a veritable hothouse of grumbling. When Kevin came in after lunch, he was a little surprised. "Have you said any of this to the pastor?" he asked. "No way!" chorused Tony and Adam. "Why would we do that?! But we are going to meet up with…"—and they named several older members of the church—"to see how we can edge the pastor out and find a better one".

———

This was a hard chapter to write because I want to speak now about perhaps one of the most common diseases to infect a church. It is a malady that causes, exacerbates and brings to crisis all manner of avoidable difficulties between the life of a pastor and the life of a church. What can cause such huge problems? A lack of openness and honesty with our pastor.

I want to commend transparent honesty and warn against pretence. Some people only speak with their pastor when they have an issue with the church leadership or a crisis in their own life. I want to encourage a broader, more normal spectrum of conversations and a resolute determination to avoid secrecy or hypocrisy.

One of the most troubled pastoral relationships in the Bible was between the apostle Paul and the lively but disorderly church in Corinth. In a most moving appeal to them, Paul writes:

> *We have spoken freely to you, Corinthians, and opened wide our hearts to you. We are not withholding our affection from you, but you are withholding yours from us. As a fair exchange—I speak as to my children—open wide your hearts also.*
>
> 2 Corinthians 6 v 11-13

> *I have spoken to you with great frankness...*
>
> 2 Corinthians 7 v 4

To have an open heart means to speak frankly without deceit or pretending. One of Paul's strongest claims is that he has done this. He has never deceived them about his life or his message but has always been open with them, in what he says and in the tender heart from which he says it. Paul cannot have been an easy leader in many ways, but he was always straight with people. What you heard was what he meant; what you saw was what you got. He pleads with them to treat him the same way. Peter similarly exhorts his readers to get rid "of all malice and all deceit [and] hypocrisy" (1 Peter 2 v 1).

Lower the drawbridge

The main focus of this chapter is to encourage openness in us as church members. But for some pastors it may come as a word in season to encourage them to "lower the drawbridge" a little so that more of their own lives and struggles are visible to the church. If you are a pastor and your church members think you have it all sorted, then you are unwittingly deceiving them. Let them into your life a bit more, and they will know that you too are a sinner in constant need of a Saviour.

Openness between church members and honesty between church members and pastors are prerequisites of a healthy church. A church in which there is hiding, secrecy and deception is a terrible parody of what the church of Jesus Christ should be. A pastor leading an honest church may face all kinds of struggles; but in the heart of such pastors there will be a powerful motivation to persevere. But a pretending church demotivates deeply; so a pastor who cannot trust the members of the church is very likely to give up and walk away.

Beware the boomerang!

Some of the most vigorous rebukes of Jesus were reserved for hypocrites. To pretend to be one thing while actually being another is destructive of true religion in a way in which few other sins are; for by appearing to be godly, hypocrites cut themselves off from the possibility of rebuke and therefore of repentance.

First and foremost, the virtue of honesty among us as church members cuts to the reality of our Christian lives. We may laugh at the wonderful parodies of hypocrisy in the Sermon on the Mount, such as the benefactors who announce their giving with triumpets, the men who "love to pray standing in the synagogues and on the street corners to be seen by others", and those taking care to look gaunt when they fast (Matthew 6 v 2, 5, 16). But our laughter has a boomerang quality; it may come back to haunt us.

Some of us may feel a particular temptation to want to impress our pastors with our godliness. If I am reading my Bible regularly (a healthy habit!), I may try to make sure my pastor sees my Bible and perhaps my Bible-reading notes, displayed casually but visibly when they visit. Or I might like to find some discreet way of letting slip about the generous gift we gave at the church gift day.

Strangely, though, those who aim to impress their pastors end up discouraging them. When our pastors stumble across some evidence of our godliness— perhaps from an off-the-cuff remark by someone quite different—they are thrilled at this evidence of grace in our lives. But not by our own shows of piety.

On the other hand, if you're like me, you may be inclined to cast a discreet veil over your failures, for fear that your pastors will think the worse of you. If we are struggling at home, perhaps, with a serious problem of anger or even domestic violence, we will not want our pastor to know. If we are being sucked into some moral compromise at work, we will steer clear of that area of conversation. If we are struggling with serious difficulties in marriage, we would hate that knowledge to spoil our pastor's idyllic picture of our family life.

Such a desire to disguise ourselves is natural but disastrous. It eats away at our hearts like a rust. And then, when there is some explosion of evil, and it all comes into the open, our pastors are devastated, since they could have no means of seeing the disaster coming. So when a marriage that kept up a front of harmony suddenly breaks down, the pastor will wish that the couple had been open, so that the love and wisdom of pastoral care could have applied prayer and the word of God to these struggles. For the church is a hospital for sick sinners; it is no place for self-righteous hypocrites. And your pastor is a doctor longing to help you beat the sickness of sin. A pastor who will think less well of you or me for our struggles with sin is not a pastor worth having in a church.

Start out in the open; then stay there

Openness is important in all the relationships between a pastor and a church. When a pastor is appointed, it is of the utmost importance that the church is honest about their expectations. What do we *really* want from our new pastor? Let us not be content with the vague waving of hands and assurances that it will all work out fine. It probably won't. Let us be professional, tie down expectations in writing, make clear contracts to define expectations, and quantify matters such as pay, housing, holidays, pensions and expenses. To clarify this much may be considered unnecessary between

Christians, but not to do so is actually dishonest and unloving. It also naïvely underestimates human sinfulness.

I hear too many stories of pastors appointed under false pretences. A church wants so much to get a particular pastor; but they are worried the pastor will not take the job. And so the job is painted in unrealistic colours. I even heard of one where the elders pretended (for that is what it was) that they only expected a certain restricted load of preaching; but when the pastor arrived, it became clear they actually wanted a much heavier load. That is dishonest—and it dishonours the Lord.

The need for openness continues when a pastor is in post, and especially when a church is under pressure. There are times in the life of most churches when membership and giving are falling, or there is particularly distressing opposition, or in some other way things do not feel good. At these times we so easily become like the people of Israel in the wilderness— who grumbled and grumbled against Moses for not giving them what they wanted.

Even the Lord Jesus faced this distressing grumbling, and had to challenge his opponents for not speaking to his face (John 6 v 41-43, 60-61). It is so much harder to speak face to face when there is disagreement. And yet it is critically important that we do. It took courage for Paul to challenge Peter face to face in Antioch; but thank God that he did (Galatians 2 v 11).

Face to face is best

In an age of quick and easy telecommunication, there are very great relational dangers with Facebook, texts and emails, to say nothing of the utterly disastrous amplifying effects of posts on Twitter or Facebook, or of emails copied to others. In an earlier age, the great nineteenth-century British evangelical, Charles Simeon, wrote this about the drawbacks even of old-fashioned letter-writing:

> *If I speak with a man, I can stop when I see it is doing harm; I can soften the truth so as not to fly in the face of his cherished views ... written words convey ideas ... but they cannot convey exact feelings ... You cannot hesitate upon paper, you cannot weep upon paper, you cannot look [with] kindness upon paper.*
>
> Churchman 114.2, p162

Let us resolve to go to the time-consuming trouble of speaking face to face when there are differences. I sometimes wish there were an emotional thermometer on emails that would prevent the message being sent if the emotional temperature was much above absolute zero. A minister friend told me of a desperate time when he was stressed and exhausted, and then received two "very critical letters from senior church members". Even though he readily admits there was some truth in their criticisms, it hurt much more for not being said face to face.

Worse still, grumbling to one another without expressing our concerns to our pastors at all risks the disastrous undermining of their leadership, as secret cabals and power groupings conspire to wrest from them the leadership entrusted to them by God. There are too many horror stories like this, perhaps especially in smaller churches. There may exceptionally be times when it is necessary for a pastor to leave a post; but how much better if that is done honestly and openly, in a context where relationships of love are sustained as carefully as they can possibly be.

So let us resolve to show towards our pastors hearts that are open, expressed in speech that is honest. And let's ask ourselves—right now—whether there are changes to make this week, to help that happen.

A prayer

Father God, I thank you for pastors who have opened their hearts to me, and to us in our church. Thank you for their honesty, their transparency and their integrity. Grant that I may open my heart to them in honest fellowship, and that we as a church may show towards them the transparency of heart and life that they have shown towards us. For Jesus' sake, Amen.

4. Thoughtful watchfulness

Will and Amy were talking over coffee at a ministry conference. Amy had just started a senior staff position as women's minister at a church. She was telling Will how they paid her to attend a women's ministry conference each January, gave her a book allowance for theological study, and had a pattern of three months' study leave for every seven years of service. She felt enthused, confident that this was a place where she could grow and develop.

Will, I'm sorry to say, did not feel like that. For eight years, he had been pastor of a small church in a downtown area. There was no conference funding, no book allowance, no sabbaticals. There was too much to be done. Or that was the message he was given. He felt stuck, stagnant inside, and that he was going nowhere in his heart. He left the conversation with Amy discouraged, and took the matter to his fellow elders.

—

We want our pastors to make progress, both in their godliness of life and in their doctrine. We do not want them to be static, stuck, stationary. We long for them to be visibly growing. And so we will want to help them to mature. Why should we do that? Let's consider these verses, written by Paul to the young man Timothy:

> *Don't let anyone look down on you because you are young, but set an example for the believers in speech, in conduct, in love, in faith and in purity ... Be diligent in these matters; give yourself wholly to them, so that everyone may see your progress. Watch your life and doctrine closely.* 1 Timothy 4 v 12-16

Paul wrote these verses to Timothy, but they apply to all pastors. So, isn't it their responsibility to make sure they do these things? Well, yes, it is. But we can help them, and we should. It is much easier for a pastor to make progress when they serve a church that expects them to make progress. A church that carelessly neglects to watch over their pastors must not be surprised to find they are not making progress.

Keep watch

How can we help our pastors? By a thoughtful watchfulness as we partner with them in keeping watch over their lives and doctrine. They keep watch over us (Hebrews 13 v 17); but there is also a sense in which we will lovingly keep watch over them. Not as prying "Big Brother" watchers, but as those who love and care for them.

There are several ways in which we can do this. In this chapter we'll think about reading, conferences, study leave, days off and vacations...

Reading: A wise pastor hopes and intends to keep up the practice of serious theological reading. Not just reading that is immediately directed to the preparation of sermons or of other Bible teaching, but reading that develops a growing depth and breadth in their understanding. This, in turn, will help them to grow in maturity as well as feeding back into their wider thinking about the direction of the church.

To give a personal example, even though I'm no longer a pastor—as I write this book, I am trying day by day to spend perhaps half an hour reading and making notes on a classic biography of Augustine of Hippo, perhaps the greatest theologian of the western part of the church of the first few centuries. I do not need to do this in order to prepare anything in particular. But it feeds my thinking, nourishes my heart and stimulates my active engagement with doctrinal questions that are as relevant today as they were in the late fourth or early fifth centuries. This kind of reading was just as valuable and nourishing when I was a pastor.

But—and here is the catch—that kind of reading is the first casualty of busyness. For several months in the last year I stopped; it was squeezed out by pressures of work.

A great way to encourage our pastors is for someone in the eldership (lay leadership) of the church to talk with them about the shape of their week, to find out about their good resolutions like this one, and then gently to do what they can to help them to keep them: "So how is the Augustine reading coming along? What are you learning?"

Conferences: Of the planning of conferences there is no end—and some of them are a weariness to the flesh. Some conferences are dire: they drain the sap out of the most lively pastor and are to be avoided like the plague. But there are plenty of good ones in which pastors will be sharpened "as iron sharpens iron" (Proverbs 27 v 17) by engagement with other pastors. At their best, these conferences can be a tremendous encouragement and stimulus to a conscientious pastor.

I used to serve with the Proclamation Trust in London, which runs conferences in the UK for serving pastors. For a number of years my wife headed up the team that runs three conferences a year for ministers' wives; these also provide encouragement out of all proportion to the time and modest expense involved. Similar movements in some other countries run comparable conferences. It is a mark of a wise church that we will gladly pay for our pastors (and, if appropriate, for ministry wives) to attend such a conference, perhaps once or even twice a year.

Study leave: Sometimes called a sabbatical, this is a common practice in academic institutions but rare elsewhere. Some churches and denominations make provision for regular periods of study leave for ministers. I have found that elders or lay leaders who themselves work, perhaps in the world of business, sometimes struggle to see the justification for this.

But my experience has been that when a church manages to shift from an inappropriate business model of the pastorate to a properly pastoral model, they learn the potential benefits. For there is a relentlessness to local church pastoral leadership that fights against prayer and quietness, and stifles serious thinking about the Bible, human nature, contemporary issues and so on. A pastor who can, from time to time, step out of the pressures of daily care for a church may stand a better chance of engaging in such reflection. When they do, the whole church will later benefit.

Study leave needs to be carefully planned, in partnership with the elders of a church; it needs to include some holiday, for pastors are often exhausted when study leave begins. But it also needs to include the kinds of study, or perhaps visits to other churches, that will refresh a pastor and bring them back raring to get back into the work of pastoral preaching, teaching and leadership.

What refreshes one pastor may not energise another. But it is important that study leave should refresh. Before my first sabbatical my elders insisted that I should *first* finish the book I was working on. I was rather cross when they said this, but later came to see the wisdom of it; my study leave refreshed me in ways it would never have done had I been slaving over the uncompleted book. By contrast, on my second sabbatical, I was simultaneously going through a breakdown and labouring (by an appropriate irony) to complete a commentary on the book of Job! Sadly, but not surprisingly, that time of leave did not give me the rest and refreshment I so clearly needed.

Days off: Keeping watch over our pastors will include some sympathetic understanding of the distinctive pressures of pastoral ministry. Some pastors can become defensively precious about the pressures they face: "Oh, it's so hard for us; you can never understand…" they say. They forget that plenty of Christian disciples face horrendous pressures, job insecurities, financial uncertaintics and health concerns. Pastors have no monopoly on pressure.

And yet there are some distinctive ways in which pastoral ministry is draining, because people in need are draining, and it is in the nature of pastoral work that it involves intensive engagement with people in great need. All Christians rub up against sadness— but pastors are required to live with grief up close and personal. When the woman with the flow of blood touched Jesus by faith, he was somehow conscious that power had gone out from him (Mark 5 v 30); there may be an analogous sense in which those who show pastoral care can feel how it drains them. Plenty of pastors can testify to this.

And so we will want to help our pastors guard the God-given boundaries of life. The one in seven Sabbath principle was given at Creation; our pastors are foolish if they think they can rise above this and work 24:7:365. And we are foolish if we collude with them in this idiocy. So we will make sure they get a proper day off, in which they are not troubled by church-leadership matters, except in the very rare cases of a true pastoral emergency. A new, young pastor spoke of his church's "strict insistence on guarding days off and holidays. It enables me," he wrote, "to work hard and rest well".

Vacations: Let us be clear about how much holiday is allowed, as every other job will be. One minister said how unhelpful it was when his church said, "Take as much as you need"; for he never really felt comfortable taking much holiday at all! Sometimes we may need to check that pastors are actually taking the holiday allowance, for there are some obsessively hard-working pastors who regularly take less than they ought.

Providing well for our pastors

Most people reading this book will have little or no say in what their pastor is paid or where they live, but it's still good to think about such things. Does the home your pastor lives in give enough space for a family (if relevant), along with somewhere quiet to pray and prepare? Is it close to any church buildings; or does it require a long commute? Is there room to show hospitality or to host a small group? In other words, does their home help them to pastor the church well?

Some pastors are paid to serve the church full-time; others are part-timers or voluntary. It's not appropriate for most of us to know exactly what our pastors are paid (any more than you would want someone quizzing you about your own salary if you have one). But neither is it right for those who serve us to be so worried about money that it limits what they can do or causes unbearable stress.

The apostle Paul tells us that those who lead the church well are worthy of honour and can reasonably expect to be paid for what they do (1 Timothy 5 v 17-18). Is there someone within your leadership team who is looking out for your pastor to make sure they get the financial support they need to pastor well? (I have written more about this in an article that you can find at www.thegoodbook.com/the-book-your-pastor-wishes-you-would-read.)

Ready to be refreshed

We want to make sure our pastors live the kind of lifestyle that any wise Christian will seek to live—with time to wind down and get enough sleep, with opportunities for regular exercise, with activities that refresh. "So what do you do to relax?" "How much sleep do you get?" "Do you take exercise?" These are all the questions of a caring church. If the answers are "I don't relax; I hardly sleep; I never get exercise", then we will want to explore with our pastors why this might be. It may be their foolishness, in which case we want to help them learn wisdom. But insofar as it may be down to preventable pressures from the church, we will want to educate one another to keep that watchful loving eye over our pastors.

The feeling of being "stuck" is deeply demotivating: "I feel trapped. I sense I am not making progress. My life seems to be ebbing away in this miserable place, with no hope of growth or development." How terrible if those dark thoughts are going round in the mind of our pastors. How much better they will pastor if we contribute to a sense that "I am growing, developing, maturing in godliness, in pastoral skills and abilities, and in wisdom. I am so thankful to serve a church who encourage me, help me and enable me so to grow."

Some of the items above, such as conferences and study leave, will need to be thought about by those in leadership in your church. But that doesn't let the rest of us off the hook! Why not stop and think, right now, about ways in which you can thoughtfully watch over your pastor to help them use their time well and wisely? This might mean asking your pastor how their holiday went or how well they are managing to take their days off. Or you could check with one of the elders/lay leaders to discover whether they pay for your pastor to go to any conferences. And if you know that your pastor is about to have time away—be that study leave, a conference or holiday—why not ask how you can pray for them? That's a simple and very practical way to be an encourager.

A prayer

Father God, thank you for the wonderful example set to me by so many pastors. Thank you for their speech, their godly conduct, their steady love, their practical faith, their zeal for purity. Thank you for their diligence and I praise you for evidence of their progress. Please help me, and help us as a church, to encourage them to keep a careful watch over themselves and their doctrine. For Jesus' sake, Amen.

5. Loving kindness

My wife, Carolyn, and I experienced practical kindness in a memorable way at one stage in our ministry. We had moved to a new place and I to a new ministry. I was happy and loving it, but my wife was deeply miserable, for all sorts of understandable reasons to which I was initially blind (how foolish and self-centred we can be).

We had worked side by side in a local church, but now my ministry was separate from where we lived, and Carolyn felt bereft of the joy of shared service. A senior member of the board to which I was accountable discovered this in a pastoral conversation with my wife; he took the trouble to ask her, and she told him! He then took practical action so that we could again serve alongside one another. It was a shining example of kindness towards a pastoral couple. We thank God for it.

—

When Paul was being brought as a prisoner to Rome, the local Christians took the trouble to walk out of the city to greet him before he even reached the city. "At the sight of these people Paul thanked God and was encouraged" (Acts 28 v 15). They didn't need to do that. It was no doubt inconvenient for some of them. It was tiring and time-consuming (and risky associating themselves with a prisoner). But it was kind. And it counted. Paul saw their kindness and, in perhaps one of the more lonely and vulnerable times of his life, he was touched and encouraged by their love.

At the very end of Acts 28 we see that Paul was able to keep ministering for another two years (v 30-31). Just as the local Christians had loved, supported and encouraged him, so Paul was enabled to keep loving, teaching and encouraging them.

2,000 years later, we can show kindness too. The parents of a pastor friend of mine were killed together one day in a car accident. In the days of trauma and grief that followed, he said to me that the church he serves had been "overwhelmingly kind". This man needed to take time off; the church gave him as much time as he needed. They gave, and went on giving, meals, cakes and thoughtful gifts. In tangible ways they let him know that they loved him. A ministry couple who lost a child in infancy gave the same testimony about their church.

These examples come from times of deep grieving, but we have plenty of everyday opportunities to be kind as well. Before you read on, why not pause for a moment and think of something kind you could do this week for your pastor or their family?

A beautiful picture of Christ's love

Kindness is a powerful and beautiful expression of the love of Christ. It is the fifth virtue I want to write about. There is no doubt in my mind that churches that show kindness will have still better pastors as a result; for it is only natural that their pastors will return to their pastoral leadership with a fresh determination to love and care for, to teach and preach to, and to pray for these who have so loved them.

If we show no kindness to our pastors, God still calls them to love, to care, to preach, to pray, and to do all their pastoral work towards us in the spirit of the Lord Jesus—who loved those who were his enemies and gave himself for them on the cross. But our pastors are not the Lord Jesus, and it is a normal and natural dynamic that if we demonstrate kindness to them, it is easier for them to give themselves gladly in caring for us.

I spoke earlier of a business mentality in church life. By this I mean the way of thinking that is always assessing strategy, methods, programmes and procedures. For this mindset the pastor is a functionary; they have a job to do, and our job as the church is to make sure that they fulfil the functions we expect of them. So, when we do a ministry review with them, we measure meetings led, sermons preached, study notes prepared, budget targets achieved, buildings renovated, and so on.

But, while there can be a place for that, perhaps the most significant things in a pastor's work are not so easily measurable—the labouring in prayer, the time-consuming and emotionally draining visits, the weeping with those who weep, the showing of the kindness of Christ to men and women as our pastors hold out to us the word of life. We want our pastors to be kind. But the opposite is also true: our kindness counts with them. We must never underestimate the significance of our simple, practical, loving kindness to our pastors.

In a revealing comment, one pastoral worker who had served first in a prosperous neighbourhood and then in a poorer area said that in the former the church was probably more professional in its approach to a fair salary, decent housing, sensible pension, and a clear system for expenses; but in the latter, while they maybe were not able to pay as much or house their staff as well, they overflowed with kindness towards them. They had time to care, and they cared. And it affected this Christian worker deeply.

How to be kind

Free babysitting, little loving gifts, flowers, practical help with a baby, weeding a garden, house-warming presents—these things are not a substitute for fair pay, decent housing, a pension, or reasonable ministry expenses. But they are not insignificant. They communicate to pastors, as to all the rest of us, that they are loved, and that is a precious gift.

Such kindness most naturally overflows to a pastor's family. If he is a married man, the way the church treats his wife is of deep significance. Some wives have chosen not to do paid jobs outside the home; they do not have to make that choice, but some choose that way of life in order to devote themselves to working alongside their husbands in hospitality and ministry of various kinds. Others work outside the home, perhaps part-time, but also give sacrificially of their time and energy to be helpers alongside their husbands in ministry.

Some have young children, some have no children, some have older children. Some have elderly parents, or parents-in-law, for whom to care. They have all the normal pressures and opportunities that the rest of us have. But alongside all of that, they want to take an active part in pastoral ministry. Let us show them we appreciate them and care for them, by the big things, like making sure there is proper pay and housing, but also in the little kindnesses that speak so eloquently of love.

Pastors are people too—and so are their children!

Pastoral homes with children are deeply affected by the love or the coldness of a church. Our own children benefitted hugely from the fun-loving kindness of a number of men and women who had the inestimable advantage of being younger than our children's parents(!) but older than our children.

In many ways being in a ministry home gave them all sorts of pluses in their childhood. I have heard many such stories of blessing from other ministry families.

But there can be downsides as well, and I have heard some darker stories. When we expect too much of our pastor's children, it can become a crushing burden for them and their parents. When they feel they are growing up in a Pharisaical goldfish bowl, being watched and judged for every misdemeanour, it is not surprising if they kick against the faith of their parents.

For the children of pastors are just as noisy, just as energetic, just as touched by sin, just as vulnerable to the pressures of culture as are all other children in Christian homes. They may or may not be true believers in their hearts; let us not assume that they are simply because they are their parents' children. Let us treat them with the kindness and understanding we would naturally extend to any other children.

One hindrance to kindness is the feeling that our pastors and their families ought to be living lives of sacrificial service to Christ. I have known churches that worry that, if they are too soft with them, their pastors may become lazy or soft in their discipleship. This—if we do feel it—is perverse. Certainly, they ought to be taking up the cross daily, saying no to self, and living lives of sacrifice for Jesus and his gospel. But so ought we and every disciple. It is one thing to make sacrifices for oneself; it's quite another to seek to impose sacrifices on others. What is more, a pastor's children, if they are not—or not yet—true believers in their hearts, will learn "Christianity" as a hard religion of imposed misery rather than a glad giving of ourselves in love for the Christ who first loved us.

(If you want to think a little more about this, I have included it in an article on pay and housing that you can find at www.thegoodbook.com/the-book-your-pastor-wishes-you-would-read.)

So let us not hesitate to pour out kindness upon our pastors, and their families if they have them. Such an eloquent expression of the love of Christ will very naturally strengthen in them a comparable kindness and love for us. Paradoxically, although we do not show kindness in order to gain benefits, we shall find ourselves pastored the better for it!

A prayer

God our Father, thank you for your overwhelming kindness to us in Jesus your Son. Thank you for so many, including so many pastors, who have been kind with the kindness of Christ to us. Grant that we may show to them something of that same kindness of Christ. For Jesus' sake, Amen.

6. High expectations

Steve and Amber had not seen one another since college. They were having a catch-up over some fast food. They are both Christians and asked one another about their churches.

"We've had a sad time," said Steve. "Last spring our pastor had an affair. He left his wife for another woman and the marriage has ended in divorce."

"Oh, I'm really sorry to hear that," said Amber. "Have you found a new pastor yet?"

"Oh, no," said Steve. "The good news is that our church are being wonderfully understanding. We are a very inclusive church. He is continuing as pastor and receiving counselling to help him through this difficult time. It is wonderful to see the church caring so much for our pastor and valuing his work so highly."

Amber was not so sure.

—

There had been an embarrassing episode at the last church council meeting. When the pastor didn't get his own way, there followed an explosive loss of temper, with shouting and some words that would better never have been said. During the following week, several of the council members were for quietly letting it all go, brushing this under the carpet, letting bygones be bygones.

But a few of them suggested that they should go and see the pastor, gently but firmly to challenge this behaviour. They did that. It was awkward—not at all an easy conversation. But, by the grace of God, the pastor went away, thought things over, and then called another church council meeting at which he publicly apologised for his loss of temper, asked for the council's forgiveness, and thanked them for caring enough for him to challenge him.

—

What are we to think when we hear these stories? I will tell you what we should think about the first one. We should think that this gets the church's value system completely upside down. No! This church does not care for their pastor and they do not value his work. On the contrary, they have very low standards and very little true love. Their apparent tolerance masks a culture that values holiness very little and esteems the pastor hardly at all, let alone his deserted wife. Pity the pastor who serves a church like this one!

By contrast, envy the pastor who serves the second church; for, although it is awkward, they really care about holiness, about the pastor's true best interests, and about the noble task of leading and serving a church.

My sixth virtue is high expectations. The opposing vice is easy-going "tolerance". The virtue and vice are paradoxical. The vice is to be easy on our pastors; the virtue is to expect the very highest standards from them.

The paradox is this: if we are easy on them, and expect little of them, our pastors will know we don't really care whether or not they do their work well. But if we expect the very highest standards of integrity and godliness from them, then they will know we care deeply about them and their work. Their job is indeed "a noble task" (1 Timothy 3 v 1), the very highest of human callings, such that, as someone once said, "Who, being a preacher, would stoop to be a king?" And, precisely because it is a noble task, it demands of its practitioners the very highest of standards.

If we know that they know that we know...

Our pastors probably came into pastoral ministry wanting to be the very best for Jesus. We will help them to be this if we, in our turn, expect this of them. For then they will know that we know that they ought to be aiming for the highest. And if we know that they know that we know this is their goal… well, it all works together for good!

Before exploring what this might mean, let me add a word of warning. We must not put our pastors on pedestals and expect them to be superhuman. Here's what the writer of Psalm 146 tells us:

> *Do not put your trust in princes, in human*
> *beings, who cannot save.*　　　Psalm 146 v 3

A pastor is a kind of "prince", one to whom is entrusted a dignity and an authority under God that is not to be despised. They have a measure of power, not least "the power of the microphone"; they stand at the front and they speak, again and again. It is therefore tempting to put them on a metaphorical pedestal, since they may need to stand on a literal pedestal or platform to speak. Psalm 146 warns us not to do this, for they are human and they are bound to disappoint us, even if only by getting sick, or old, or dying. They cannot save, and we must not expect them to. There is only one who can save—the Lord Jesus Christ.

Some years ago, when a prominent preacher in my country fell tragically into a terrible sin, from which he has not repented, a friend of mine commented that it reminded him of this verse, "Do not put your trust in princes". Because he had been such an extraordinarily gifted preacher, some of us had perhaps slipped into that trap; "If only this man can preach for us, then all will be well," we may have thought.

Paid and protected

So what does it mean to hold our pastors to the highest standards? Paul teaches about this in his first letter to Timothy, in the same passage where he says that they are worthy of double honour if they labour in preaching and teaching (1 Timothy 5 v 17-18). Paul goes on to say, "Do not entertain an accusation against an elder unless it is brought by two or three witnesses" (v 19). In other words, our pastors should be paid properly and protected from false accusations.

A church leader is particularly vulnerable to rumours, gossip and false accusations, especially in our litigious age. Paul invokes a principle from Old Testament law, which said that an accusation must be properly checked and double-checked, to make sure it is really true.

So, when we hear a tidbit of gossip about our pastor, how should we respond? Check that it's true. "So, who did you hear this from? Have you spoken to the pastor directly about this to check it out? No? Well, then you are joining in with malicious gossip. So, how about you and I meet the pastor and say we have heard this rumour? Let's see what explanation there might be."

Hold them to the highest

But what if it is true? What if, when it is properly investigated, we find that our pastor has sadly fallen into some scandalous ungodliness—perhaps some financial irregularity with their expenses, or some emotional or even sexual involvement that is unfaithful to their marriage, or an explosive temper outburst, or an episode (or even pattern) of drunkenness, or colluding in some political manoeuvring in church life? What then? Paul goes on to tell us: "But those elders who are sinning you are to reprove before everyone, so that the others may take warning" (1 Timothy 5 v 20).

Presumably, this is after a private conversation (as Jesus taught in Matthew 18 v 15-17), and only if the sin needs to be brought out into the open in a church meeting. But what a painful thing this will be, and how hard to do it! So Paul goes on to insist, "I charge you, in the sight of God and Christ Jesus and the elect angels, to keep these instructions without partiality, and to do nothing out of favouritism" (v 21). This is very, very important. Our pastors need to be held accountable in love. They are sinners just like us, and they will only know that we love them and value their "noble task" if we hold them to the highest.

For pastors are vulnerable to particular sins. Like the otherwise unknown Diotrephes, whom we meet in John's third letter, they may "love to be first" (3 John 9); they may revel in the prominence they enjoy, and need to be gently rebuked for their over-sensitivity to criticism, or their reluctance to delegate and truly to entrust ministry tasks to others in church. Or they may become bossy, "lording it" over church members (1 Peter 5 v 3). Or they may seek praise from people (John 5 v 44). Or love the honour that may come to them, or do what they do in order for people to see their religious fervour (Matthew 23 v 5-7). In all these and other ways, our pastors need us to hold them to the highest.

One of the most sensitive and difficult matters in the life of a church is knowing how to hold our pastors to the highest standards in love. It is fraught with danger. We ourselves very easily slip into hypocrisy or self-righteousness, thanking God that we are not as bad as our terrible pastor. We may use such a process as an excuse to get our own back on a pastor who has not treated us as we feel we deserve to have been treated. We may be reluctant to forgive when a pastor repents, or to restore him into Christian fellowship (even if leadership may no longer be appropriate for him).

But however difficult it is, our pastors will not know that we truly value their work unless we are determined to hold them to the very highest standards of godliness. I remember shocking the church I served by saying once, in a sermon, "If I have an affair, I hope you will love me enough to put me out of fellowship until I repent, and to stand me down from being your pastor". But it was true; I did hope that. I would hate to serve a church who didn't care about my godliness. And the mere fact that I knew that fellowship did care helped me to guard my own life and doctrine. Strange and paradoxical as it may seem, I served the church all the better for knowing that they had high expectations.

A prayer

Almighty God, our holy and heavenly Father, I bow before you in the burning purity of your holiness. Thank you that your love for us is a holy love, and your promise to us is that we will be conformed by your Holy Spirit to the purity of your holy Son. Thank you that you care so deeply about the moral holiness of our pastors. Grant that, as a church, we may hold our pastors to the very highest standards, so that the penitence and godliness they exemplify to us may set the tone in our churches for the penitence and godliness they too expect from us. For Jesus' sake, Amen.

7. Zealous submission

Robin was in his eighties now. The new pastor was the fifth he had known. Robin loved the way the church served university students and directed their resources towards reaching them and building them up in Christ. It was a tremendous work. When the new pastor drew the church's attention to the gospel poverty of the large local school, Robin had a bit of an inward struggle. He loved the university student work and had an emotional and historical affinity with it. The new pastor wanted to invest precious resources in a gospel schools' worker. But Robin knew that he was not the pastor, and that the pastor's proposal was a perfectly valid gospel priority. So, rather wonderfully and graciously, when it came to the meeting, he gave the pastor's leadership his full support.

—

Jeremy, Angela and Mike had been senior members of the church for many years. They had seen pastors come and pastors go. They rather liked the sense that they— as a group who were looked up to as the experienced old-timers—were the real power in the church.

When the new, young pastor came, he led the church in a careful review of the gospel needs in the area, with wide consultation and some good times of corporate prayer, at the end of which, he proposed that the church prune some of the ministries that didn't seem to be reaching non-Christians at all, and develop a deliberate and intentional focus on reaching the large population of mainly Islamic immigrants in the area.

Many, even most, of the church members could see that this was a strong gospel decision. In their hearts, Jeremy, Angela and Mike could see that too. But it had not been their idea, and they resented it. When it came to the decision-making meetings, the full weight of their seniority—and indeed their effective power of veto—were brought to bear to stop this initiative. The pastor felt discouraged and frustrated.

—

My final virtue is this: let the pastor lead and be zealous in following the direction of that leadership (so long as it is in a gospel direction)! Our pastors serve us by leading us, by "directing the affairs of the church well" (1 Timothy 5 v 17). We are to "submit to their authority" (Hebrews 13 v 17; see also 1 Peter 5 v 5).

Submission is deeply countercultural because our innate sinfulness makes us desperately reluctant to submit to anyone. The Bible teaches various different forms of submission, including that of citizens to civil authorities, wives to husbands (a particularly easy one to misunderstand and caricature but beautiful when done rightly), children to parents, slaves to masters (albeit condemning slavery as a terrible institution) and church members to pastors. These kinds of submission are all different, but each is, in some way, an expression of submission to God.

Submission of church members to pastors, like the other kinds of submission above, can never be absolute. Absolute authority is given to Christ alone, and no human authority—a tyrannical government, an unjust employer, a domineering husband, an abusive parent or a controlling pastor—should ever be allowed to usurp that good authority of Christ. But there is an authority that is proper to pastors.

Is your pastor an employee—or a shepherd?

One way in which this is subverted is when the unpaid leadership of a church view the pastor as an employee: "We are employing you to do certain tasks for us. You are accountable to us. You report to us." While churches configure their leadership in different ways, and will usually have some healthy form of shared leadership, we must not forget that the New Testament picture of pastors is that they follow the pattern of Jesus, the great Pastor (= Shepherd); they serve the flock by leading.

When we call a pastor, we call a leader who is accountable to Christ, the great Shepherd, and not primarily to us. Even with shared leadership, we should let the one entrusted with senior leadership actually lead.

We are given a beautiful insight into the purpose of a pastor's authority in a tiny little comment that Paul makes about the leader of—presumably—a house church in Corinth. Speaking of "the household of Stephanas" who had "devoted themselves to the service of the Lord's people", he writes, "I urge you … to submit to such people and to everyone who joins in the work and labours at it" (1 Corinthians 16 v 15-16). We do not know if Stephanas was exactly what we would call a pastor. But the principle is there: here are people who are active in the work of the gospel; they labour at it; and Paul says the others in Corinth would do well to submit to them and those like them.

In a similar way, we need our pastors to lead us in the work of the gospel of Christ, and should want to support them zealously in this.

Pulling together

The partnership between a pastor and a local church is a gospel partnership. We see a similar partnership between the apostle Paul and the church in Philippi. "In all my prayers for all of you, I always pray with joy because of your partnership in the gospel" (Philippians 1 v 4-5). The apostle and the Christians in Philippi pulled together in the service of the gospel of Jesus. In the same way, pastors and church members are to work alongside one another for the promotion of the good news of the Lord Jesus Christ.

Leadership is a difficult thing but very important. Every school, each business, and government after government know just how important it is. You watch a failing school transformed by new leadership and can see the impact it can have. It is the same with a church. Leadership is to be plural; it ought never to be an individual tyranny. But there does need to be a senior leader, however committed to shared leadership they may be. It's not an easy task for a leader to bring a church family with them to share a vision and engage energetically in it. But it is a great thing when it happens—when a senior pastor so engages a church in a vision that the whole church labour with glad zeal to fulfil it.

How's your vision?

There are bad visions—visions in which the church leader's fame and comfort are being served, visions in which the pride of the church is puffed by their "success", visions in which a church luxuriates in comfortable success, enjoyable meetings and being praised by everyone. Such evil visions are not what I am talking about. I am talking about gospel visions—visions that long for the glory of Jesus through the proclamation of his gospel and the building up of a local church committed to prayer, to the gospel and to living lives among their neighbours that are driven by, and consistent with, the gospel.

But within that umbrella definition, there are different ways a church can choose to prioritise its energies. It is here that the challenge of the pastor's leadership is engaged. Some people are dreamers and visionaries who find it deeply uncongenial to sign up for another's leadership; they always want their church to be pursuing their particular version of the gospel vision. They will be a pain in the pastor's neck.

Like Absalom—who sneakily undermined King David's authority and took it for himself (2 Samuel 15 v 1-6)—we would be sowing seeds of discord, if we privately suggested to people that the church would be a better place if our way was followed.

Of course, some pastors exacerbate this problem by being oversensitive or too busy to listen. A secure pastor will gladly open up different possibilities in discussion, hear them all, and lead the church leadership in prayerful discernment of God's best way forward. Our challenge comes when the outcome of this prayer and discussion is not the way we would have chosen.

I am not speaking about visions that are ungodly, for then we may need to leave a church as a matter of conscience. But most of the time, it does not come to that. It is simply that our particular ideas—for pursuing this ministry or that ministry—have not won a consensus among the leadership. We need to learn gladly to submit to the gospel authority of our pastors as they lead our churches. And not just to submit negatively—resolving not to cause trouble—but to submit gladly and energetically, engaging our energies with zeal in playing our part in pursuing a gospel vision that may not have been our first choice.

Absalom or apathy?

A church full of Absaloms is pretty demotivating for a pastor, who must then spend so much time and energy fire-fighting. But a church full of dull apathy is equally demotivating, for the pastor feels that unless they do the pushing and pushing and pushing, nothing will ever move. And that's a tough call too.

But imagine a church who get behind a shared vision, led by a godly pastor, each resolving to push with all the zeal and energy the Lord inspires, and all in the same direction! That is a wonderful church to serve. A pastor in that kind of church will not be tempted to look around to see if a transfer can be arranged to a more united and zealous church. Let's resolve to be the kinds of church members who promote that kind of zealous glad submission to our pastors.

When your pastor looks at you, do you think they see this kind of zealous glad submission? If they do, thank the Lord for enabling you to respond in this way. If they don't, what will you do this week to start to change that, so that you're not just submitting negatively, but gladly and enthusiastically following the vision they have set?

At the end of Paul's letter to the church in Rome there is the longest of all his lists of greetings (Romans 16 v 1-16, 21-23). He greets twenty-five named people and an unknown number of others, and he sends them greetings from eight people. One theme that comes through in all these greetings is the number of brothers and sisters who have worked hard for the Lord Jesus, or who are described as "workers". Clearly their glad hard work warmed the heart of the apostle, as it will warm the heart of any pastor today.

A prayer

Father God, thank you for the prayerful gospel initiatives taken by our pastors. Help them always to conform their leadership to your word in every way. And, when they do, grant us grace gladly to follow and eagerly to participate in the gospel work in which they lead us. For Jesus' sake, Amen.

Somebody needs to know your pastor!

This chapter is not for everybody. But in each church it will be for two or three somebodies. The senior people in your church ought to have a think about whose responsibility it will be to know the pastor well. It might be the other elders, or—if there is a large eldership—a few selected elders. Perhaps it is some other senior lay leaders. I suggest that two or three is a good number.

Decide who they are and then entrust to them the privilege and responsibility of getting to know the pastor really well, on behalf of the whole church. They will be a kind of pastor's pastoral-support group. They can then act as a bridge between the pastor and the whole church when questions arise about how the whole church can care for the pastor. If you are part of a large church with a staff team, different elders, deacons or members of the church may be assigned this task for different staff members.

—

To be a little provocative, you might like to imagine a new game. It's a variation of "Mr and Mrs", in which a couple are asked questions to test how well they know one another. The results can be embarrassing. Let's call this game "Pastor and People". A pastor is asked questions about the church members, and then the pastor's pastoral-support group are asked how well they know their pastor. It's the second part that concerns me now. How well do you know your pastor? And would the ignorance be embarrassing?

—

Come back with me to the pastors' hall of faith from chapter 1 (page 13). We met there pastors with different backgrounds, varied personalities and all manner of strengths and weaknesses. Where would you find your pastor(s) in this hall? How well do you know them?

Here are a few questions that may help you get to know them better: to think yourself into their shoes, their mind, their heart, their hopes, their anxieties, their fears, their goals, their skin. You know in theory that they are fully human beings, like you—at least, I hope you do. But you may not have given much thought to what that means.

A. How will family background and childhood home have shaped your pastor's hopes and aspirations?

All of us are shaped by our families; our pastors are no different. They, like you, instinctively wanted to do something that would make their parents—perhaps especially a father—proud. So think about how this might now feel for your pastor.

What do you know about their family background and upbringing? If not much, why not get to know them a bit better and find out? And then think how that background might affect their hopes and aspirations, and shape their fears and anxieties.

B. What models of pastoral ministry has your pastor known up until now? What constitutes "success"?

Every pastor holds in their mind an idea of what a "successful" ministry looks like. Although that mental picture ought to be shaped by Scripture, it is filled out and gains concrete substance in ministries they have seen and known. Under what kind of ministry, in what sort of church, did they first come to a saving faith in Christ? That will shape them deeply. What sort of leadership saw them grow, mature and develop in their discipleship of Jesus? That too will form their expectations significantly.

Think about your pastor. Find out a bit more about the models of ministry that have influenced them. Compare these to the context in which they are serving now. How might the similarity or the contrast between present ministry and influential models affect them today?

C. What material lifestyles has your pastor (and spouse, if married) known up until now?

It is all too easy, and sometimes downright trite, to mouth the right phrases about making sacrifices for Christ and his gospel. In the drama of a moment of wholeheartedness, all of us have thought, and said, and meant, dramatic and radical things about how willing we are to give up everything for Jesus. At least, I hope we have. It is a sad sort of Christian who has never made these kinds of pledges in their heart.

It is a very different matter to live it out in the myriad little decisions we all make about lifestyle. In many ways, the really big question is: what sort of lifestyle have we been accustomed to? It is much easier not to run a car if we have never owned a car, to dress cheaply if we have always bought plain clothes, to live simply if we have always lived near the minimum.

But many of us, and that includes many pastors, have enjoyed much more than what we and they really need. And that makes financial sacrifice hurt a lot more. It doesn't make it wrong—it may be very right (for us, just as much as for our pastors)—but it makes it harder. And if we are to understand our pastors, and what it feels like to be in their skin, we need to know what material lifestyle they enjoyed in the past.

So try to find out about your pastor's childhood, about their life before being called to the pastorate, about the lifestyles enjoyed by their brothers and sisters, and the cousins of their children, if they have them. Are they used to running a car? Two cars? What make of car? What kind of holidays are they used to?

What sort of houses did they live in before entering pastoral ministry? And where? What quality of schools did they go to? Do they have nephews or nieces? If so, where do their children's cousins live and what sort of schools do they go to? What kind of digital gadgetry would they have been used to? The latest model of the trendiest smartphone? Or what?

How does this pattern of past "normal" compare with their lifestyle now? I am not saying that now ought to match the past; it may be good and right that it doesn't. But you will never know what it feels like to be in your pastor's skin if you do not grasp the expectations they have inherited.

D. What kind of person is your pastor?

Of each member of the pastoral staff, ask the question: *what sort of person is he or she?* I mean in temperament, personality and interests. Are they more towards the introvert or extrovert ends of the spectrum? Do people energise them or drain them? Do they thrive in large groups or shrivel up with a shy desire to escape? Are they steady in mood, or more up-and-down sorts of people, prone to low mood, sometimes a bit "hyper", or what? Does artistic creativity get their juices flowing? Are they musical? Does drama energise them? Or sport—and, if so, what sports? What, if anything, do they like to read (apart from what is needed for ministry)? What do they like to watch in movies or on television?

How well do you know them? Try to get a better feel for their personality, their interests. What do they love to talk about when it's not a work thing? What energises them and what drains them?

E. If your pastor is a married man, what does his wife think about his work, and about being married to a pastor?

I mean, really think. She may say the right things and smile at the appropriate times. But what does she really think and feel, deep down. Did she marry a pastor, or was this a later change in their marriage? If so, did she welcome it or does she have mixed feelings? Why? How might this impact the daily feel and morale of life for the pastor? Are there some senior women in the church who make it their responsibility to get alongside the pastor's wife and really get to know her? You can apply the same scrutiny to the husbands of women on your pastoral staff. Try to enter imaginatively into how the dynamics of expectations in marriage might impact both husband and wife.

How well do you know your pastor?

I hope you feel you have at least the beginnings of an imaginative understanding of what gets your pastor out of bed in the morning, or indeed what might make them reluctant to start the day's work. You will probably have as many gaps as you have insights, but at least you are beginning to ask these questions.

If you are anything like me—before I became a pastor—it may never have occurred to you to ask these questions. I wish someone had prompted me to do this back then.

A prayer

Father God, thank you that you know our pastor fully, and that you are working in their life to make them more like Christ. Please help some of our church family to get to know our pastor well enough that we can love them better and support them more effectively as they seek to give a godly lead to our church. For Jesus' sake, Amen.

CONCLUSION:

Where do we go from here? How can we turn things around?

So how are things in your church? Is it a church marked by a joyful gospel partnership between the pastor and church members? Or not? How well do you know your pastor?

I have found writing this a challenge to myself, as I have written about virtues that I am deeply conscious I do not possess in sufficient measure, and vices that I can see all too clearly in my own life and on my own lips. The experience of thinking through these things has moved me to repentance in some areas, and caused me to resolve to be more the kind of church member who will energise and cheer my pastor so that their work is truly a joy and not a burden (Hebrews 13 v 17). What about you?

It may be that your church is one which supports and encourages the pastor really well. I have known many churches like this, both as pastor, as a member and as an observer from a distance. If so, all well and good—although it might be worth quietly checking with your pastor that they agree with your good assessment!

For some, things may be so bad that drastic action needs to be taken. I know of churches where a core of long-serving, powerful, perhaps older members hold on to power and make the life of a minister miserable. For some of you elders or church-council members, church secretaries or treasurers, the most positive thing you can do is graciously to step down and give support from the "backbenches". You may find your reluctance to do this has more to do with a love of status and, yes, even power, than you want to admit. But take the bull by the horns and do it—and do it soon!

Or maybe you see this happening, and you want to support your pastor against just such a core of powerful members. You can help to guard what is right by speaking up in support of your pastor and stating your intention to follow where they lead. Sometimes all it takes is for four or five church members to say, "Our pastor is our pastor, and he has been prayerful and wise, and we will follow his leadership, and so should we all" to break the power of a group wanting to destroy his vision.

In extreme cases, it may be advisable for a pastor or minister to move on. Too much has been said that cannot be unsaid, and a fresh start for all concerned may be the best—or the least worst—option. If that is to happen, guard carefully against a root of bitterness, either in the leaving pastor or the church. Do not give the devil a foothold. Take care and time and trouble to ask for and to give forgiveness, and to part with Christian love.

For many churches, and in some denominations or associations of independent churches, there may be the possibility of bringing in some outside figure—a senior former pastor, a moderator, another presbyter, a bishop—by mutual agreement to help a church and a pastor work through difficulties together in a spirit of Christ-like repentance and with a mutual desire to do better. That can be a wise and godly way forward.

But, whatever your circumstances, whatever the past, whatever the present relationships between pastor and members, do something. Either do something to put right what is wrong. Or do something to guard what is right. The devil is constantly prowling around. He loves to cause discord between church leaders and church members; it is a very effective way of damaging the work of the gospel. We must do all we can to resist him, standing firm in faith.

So here's a suggestion: why not get your church members, or perhaps the leadership team, to read through this book over a few weeks and then discuss each section with a view to prayer and (if necessary) change? You will, no doubt, come up with other examples, other ideas, other and perhaps better ways of responding. If you are very brave, you might even get together with your pastor to ask them what in this book they would really like you to take on board, even if they might be embarrassed to ask!

You will not be able to put right everything that is wrong. But do something. Identify one step that you can take as a church to care better for your pastor. And it's a long-term project. What we need is a shift of church mindset so that caring for our pastors becomes an integral and normal part of what we do.

And please pray for your pastors. As the American preacher Robert E. Harris once said: if you want a better pastor, you can get one by praying for the one you already have!

A prayer

Father God, thank you for the promise of the Lord Jesus to build his church. Thank you that the victorious and ascended Jesus has given pastor-teachers to his church. Help us as a church to know how better to support and care for our pastor, that they may more joyfully pastor us and so that honour may come to the Lord Jesus in every way. In Jesus' name, Amen.

Acknowledgements

Although I wanted to write this book, I did not find it easy. The principles are not complex, but the practical outworking is so varied, depending upon culture, church government and subculture, and so very many personal factors. The result is inevitably coloured by my experience and those of others in ministry whom I know. I hope it will at least get conversations started among church members. The process of thinking through these matters has brought home to me that I have not always shown these virtues myself, since leaving local church pastoral leadership. I am resolved to do better and hope this book may help others to make similar resolutions.

I am grateful to many, whether in pastoral ministry or not, who have shared parts of their stories with me from time to time. A number of my former students from the Cornhill Training Course have been particularly insightful. I am especially thankful to Graham Beynon, Auriel Schluter and Declan Flanagan for helping to point me in some helpful directions. Alison Mitchell, my editor, has been thoughtfully encouraging and wonderfully insightful throughout. My wife, Carolyn, has been her usual unfailingly supportive and insightful self; I am grateful to her for every book I manage to complete.

Christopher Ash

A practical guide to listening to sermons

Much more is involved in truly listening to Bible teaching than just sitting there. Christopher Ash outlines seven ingredients for healthy listening. He then deals with how to respond to bad sermons—ones that are dull, inadequate or heretical—and then challenges us with ideas for encouraging our Bible teachers to give sermons that will really help us to grow as Christians.

thegoodbook
COMPANY

BIBLICAL | RELEVANT | ACCESSIBLE

At The Good Book Company, we are dedicated to helping Christians and local churches grow. We believe that God's growth process always starts with hearing clearly what he has said to us through his timeless word—the Bible.

Ever since we opened our doors in 1991, we have been striving to produce Bible-based resources that bring glory to God. We have grown to become an international provider of user-friendly resources to the Christian community, with believers of all backgrounds and denominations using our books, Bible studies, devotionals, evangelistic resources, and DVD-based courses.

We want to equip ordinary Christians to live for Christ day by day, and churches to grow in their knowledge of God, their love for one another, and the effectiveness of their outreach.

Call us for a discussion of your needs or visit one of our local websites for more information on the resources and services we provide.

Your friends at The Good Book Company

thegoodbook.com | thegoodbook.co.uk
thegoodbook.com.au | thegoodbook.co.nz
thegoodbook.co.in